ARE YOU JOKING, JEREMIAH?

By NORMAN C. HABEL

CONCORDIA PUBLISHING HOUSE
St. Louis, Missouri

812.54

H11a

105412

July 1978

Fifth Printing 1970

Published by
Concordia Publishing House, St. Louis, Missouri
Concordia Publishing House Ltd., London, E. C. 1
© 1967 Walther League

Library of Congress Catalog Card No. 67-24414

MANUFACTURED IN THE UNITED STATES OF AMERICA

CONTENTS

MEET JEREMIAH

This book is an opportunity to meet Jeremiah. It's a chance for you to take the risk and resurrect that famous prophet of doom. He leaps out at you from the strange world of the Old Testament. Of course, you may resurrect a few other things as well, as you hear your own generation talking and your Lord talking back.

Kids with a wild imagination can meet Jeremiah by reading this book to themselves. But this text is not only meant to be read alone. It's supposed to be lived and experienced with others.

So don't just sit there. Get up and read it aloud, act it out, yell it out, fling the words back and forth, sing it, introduce it on Sunday morning. But above all, live it with others. That's the way to do it. Just ask the kids from Luther Memorial Church in St. Louis, who first lived through it with me.

Don't be surprised if Jeremiah speaks about jeans and cokes and other modern items. The prophet is jumping out of the past to speak with us today. We have moved the clock forward. And don't be alarmed if some words take on fresh meanings. A word like *sacrament*, for example, is used not only in the traditional sense of a rite which Jesus Christ has instituted as a means of grace but also in the broader sense of special means which God may use to get through to men of faith. Listen to the word and let God use you to get through to others. Okay? Then speak up, Jeremiah. We're with you.

The Plan of This Book

When you read this book, you will meet other characters besides Jeremiah. Kids like yourselves will have their say. Our Lord will address you and confide in you. In short, the plan of each chapter is an follows:

Part One: An Experience in Three Parts

First, The Prophet! Jeremiah the prophet on the loose with a message.

Second, The Kids! Kids saying what they think about Jeremiah's pitch.

Third, The Lord! Our Lord's answer to the kids' rather sassy lines.

Part Two: A Related Form of Worship

If you plan to sit down and read this book to meet Jeremiah, we suggest that you skip part two of each chapter. But if you do that, you are not being fair to yourself or to Jeremiah. If you want to experience the full jar of Jeremiah's message, follow one of the suggestions below.

Ways to Use This Book

a. *Dramatic Reading:* Using two or more good readers present the message of Jeremiah in part one of each chapter to your gang. Then chew it over, fight about it, and conclude with the worship presentation given in part two of the chapter.

b. *Dramatic Reading with Music:* We have found that a creative guitarist, for example, can play appropriate music as the text is read with sensitivity and punch. The musician should study the text to find sounds which capture the mood of the text and the reader. The refrain of "Are You Joking, Jeremiah?" is to be found italicized and indented in the lines of the kids. The tune for this song is given in the back of the book. The refrain for Chapter Four is sung to the tune of "Hang Down Your Head, Tom Dooley."

c. *Dramatic Reading in Church:* By presenting one or two chapters of this material in a regular Sunday worship service teen-agers can speak God's Word with their congregation. Some congregations prefer to have a dramatic portrayal of this nature after the opening hymn. The liturgy can then proceed without interruption.

d. *Dramatic Reading with Folk Songs:* Appropriate folk songs can be sung at the beginning or end of many sections. In Chapter Three, for example, Dotty Haecker, one of the finest folk singers I have heard, began with "Go Tell It on the Mountain." After the reference to "400 miles" she broke into a few lines of "Five Hundred Miles" and employed that tune in the background. She ended Jeremiah's message with "The Eve of Destruction." For the kids' section the refrain of "Are You Joking, Jeremiah?" provided the song. During much of the Lord's answer in Chapter Three she played variations on "Healing River" and concluded with a verse or two of that song. Guitarists and singers can work out their own song associations.

e. *Dramatic Portrayal:* The message of these presentations can have even greater impact if the lines are learned by heart and the text dramatized. The lines of each chapter can be divided into parts for Jeremiah, God, the kids, and the Lord. The kids' parts can be broken into paragraphs and spoken by several teen-agers. If a group desires, it can use a small speech chorus to speak some of the lines of Jeremiah or the Lord to break these longer sections. A creative director will sense the best way to use these materials in his group.

f. *Dramatic Reading and Study:* After a dramatic presentation with a group of teen-agers, college kids, or adults, a discussion of the material is often helpful.

The major Biblical texts on which the chapters of the book are based are cited below.

Chapter One —

"On Call"
Jer. 1:4-10 (compare Is. 6)
Jer. 23:18-22
Matt. 28:16-20

Chapter Two —

"Signs of the Times"
Jer. 1:11-16; 13:12-14
Jer. 4:5-8, 19-28
Jer. 25:15-17
Matt. 26:36-46; 26:26-29

Chapter Three —

"Such Antics"
Jer. 13:1-11; 19:1-11
Jer. 27:1-7; 28:1-11
Jer. 16:1-9 (compare Hos. 1)
Jer. 17:1; 13:23
Matt. 21:12-13; Luke 7:11-17
John 1:1-18

Chapter Four —

"Hang Down Your Head, Jeremiah"
The Confessions of Jeremiah
in Jer. 11:18 — 12:6; 15:15-21;
17:14-18; 18:18-23; 20:7-18
Matt. 10:16-23, 34-42

Chapter Five —

"Let's Celebrate"
Jer. 38 and 32
Jer. 30:10-17; 31:15-20
Jer. 31:31-34 especially
Luke 22 — 24

You may find other ways to use this book. Above all, give Jeremiah a chance to come alive. Meet him head on. But don't ignore him. He's your kind of man.

part one

CHAPTER ONE

ON CALL

Prophet:
Some years ago,
When I was young,
In the middle of my teens,
Sporting jeans
Or lounging on the rooftops
Back in Israel,
My life began to drag.

My hopes were dull,
As dismal as Sheol,
That dungeon of the dead,
That cavern underground,
Yawning up at God
And defiantly exposing
Its black and murky seas inside,
Where everything is limp
And lifeless.

My name is Jeremiah,
Or Jerry, if you like,
And my father was a priest,
Which doesn't really matter
In the least,
Except that when I was a boy,
I had no beat,
I had no go,
No gang where I belonged,
Like some boys that I know.

I had no number I could dial,
No football and
No groove,
Until a frightening message
Was delivered to my house
By my God.
Yes, by God,
My God called Yahweh,
Lord of Hosts!

That day
Was like the day
When scared young lovers
First permit the magic touch
Of tender, powdered skin,
Sensitized by love,

To stir the nerves of life
Within.

Yes, I was scared,
As scared as you, my friend,
When you don't know just what to do
With a screaming in your head.

For on that day
God summoned me
To stand before His council
Filled with fearsome heavenly beings
In a sapphire heavenly court
Alight with shimmering glory
And hear His bold decree.

When you look around that council,
You can see swift cherubim
Like snarling golden sphinxes
With flickering golden wings.

The weirdest things!

And you can see tall messengers of heaven
Poised to parachute to earth
Like silver lightning bolts
Or flying horsemen riding down
On long, white laser beams
That reach the ground.

But no one left the court,
And no one disappeared from sight
In the clouds that clothed the earth
That night.

At last the Lord addressed me
To my face
In a shrill magnetic voice
That dragged me from my corner
To the hot seat
In the forecourt of the council.

"Young man," He said,
"I've chosen you
For a difficult assignment
To be My new ambassador
At large
To the people of your land.

"Since you were but an embryo,
My hands have worked on you
Like a sculptor
Or a potter at his wheel,
To mold your will
With unseen skill
So that you will be a true man,
The one who stands for Me,
Stands up for Me
And tries to understand for Me
What I am doing on the earth."

But I said, "God,
There must be some mistake.
I can't do work like that.
After all,
I'm only in my teens
Sporting jeans
And lounging on the rooftops.
I've had no training
In diplomacy
Or politics,
In how to speak,
Or how to pray in public.

"You'll soon be sorry, God,
If You pick someone like me.
Well, God?
Well, can't You see?"

But God thinks He is God,
Which isn't very odd,
I guess.
And He doesn't hold
With kids like me
Telling Him His job,
I guess.

Then God replied,
"Keep quiet, son,
Don't answer Me like that.
Don't say you're only in your teens,
For you will go
Wherever I decide,
And you will say
The words which I supply.

"Don't be afraid
Of anyone at all,
For they are just as scared as you
If you could see inside
Their hardening hearts
And hardening arteries.

"And more than that,
Don't be afraid to fail,
As most men seem to be,
For I am with you
Even when you do.
Yes, I am,
I AM.

"Stand up then, Jeremiah!
Stand up and be a man!"

The court of heavenly beings
Sat silent, cold and strained,
As God stretched forth
His slender, flickering hand
To lash my lip
As with a whip
Or with a cattle brand.

"My words," said God,
"Have filled your mouth
And loosened up your tongue
Like acids will
When you have had your fill
Of something very sharp.

"That's all you really need!

"Now, go!

"Go off and win the world.
Make its history out of date
By changing men
And rearranging fate
With words that I provide.

"With violent words!

"You heard!

"Your role is first ambassador
To tell this squirming world
That I am flinging justice
At every evil nation
To straighten out the mess.

"Now, go!"

So off I went
To break the world,
To make it spin
And reel
Just like a bitten eel.

For I was now a man of God,
A messenger with power in my words
To mold the might of nations
According to a plan
Unknown to man—
Or so I thought.

I hope you understand!

Well, do you?

Kids:
Are you joking, Jeremiah?
Are you poking fun at us?
God doesn't talk with teen-age kids
Like that!
He doesn't summon them
Before His heavenly throne
With foolish calls
Like that!

Your imagination, Jeremiah,
May be something tough,
But you can't ask a kid today
To say
Okay
And swallow stuff like that.

Are you joking, Jeremiah?
Are you poking fun at us?
God doesn't talk with teen-age kids,
With kids like us, like that.

He doesn't summon them
Before His heavenly throne,
He doesn't summon kids like us
With foolish calls like that.

Your way of thinking, Jeremiah,
Is very much old hat.
You just can't ask a kid today
To say okay
And swallow stuff like that.

Your line sounds like our TV shows
When men invade the sky
Or some strange zone
Far from outer space,
Where no one ever flies
And no one really tries.

But cherubim with wings
Or unseen messengers from God
Are just too much!

And if they are around,
They never show their faces anymore.
Of that we're rather sure
When we're lying on the rooftops
Or lying on the floor
Like dreamy Jeremiah.

We don't see God extend His hand
Electrifying lips
And sending men on trips
To earth.

Our world is very different,
We flip a switch
And flip a pizza in the oven,
But nothing ever happens
To tune God in,
Come love or sin
In 1972
No matter what we do
Even with a telescope
Or two!

Are you joking, Jeremiah,
Or do you have a reason
For saying that you sat
In a glowing council hall of angels
All around God's throne —
Like that?

Are you really on the level
When you claim the Word of God
Is riding on your lips
To make the nations fall
And crumble?

After all!

Your claim is quite preposterous,
It simply wouldn't work
If you tried to change
The kids today
With weird old words,
To say nothing of a nation
Like China or America,
Who are always crossing swords.

Are you joking, Jeremiah?
Why mention that you sat
With angels all around God's throne,
To kids like us, like that?

Are you really on the level
When you claim the Word of God
Upon your lips can make a nation fall?
Now after all!

Your claim is quite preposterous.
It simply wouldn't work.
If you tried to change the kids today
With words I say,
They'd label you a jerk.

We cannot even get our parents
To try and understand
The rights and roles
Of teen-age men
In this great, new generation
Of love and fun.

Your call still makes no sense to us.

Absolutely none!

Your call seems much the same to us
As if a high school principal we know
Told us to fly a horse
To intercept a rocket,
Or pull a pencil from our pocket
To sign a bill
And buy the U. S. from the devil.

The plot was really great,
But it's simply out of date!

Your call!

It's laughable!
It's ludicrous!
It simply doesn't work
To execute a plan of God,
Whom no one else can see,
With nothing else but words —
Weird words!

The Lord:
If you'll pardon My intrusion
In your rather flip response,
The way you kids object to calls
Like those of Jeremiah

23

Sounds just like any prophet did
Before he caught on fire
With the words I spoke in him
Centuries ago.

If you could only hear —
Believing,
Hoping,
Doubting —
The call which comes right now.

This call I send is from a mountain
High in Galilee,
Where all of My disciples met —
Believing,
Hoping,
Doubting —
After I had risen!

Your task is very much the same
As that of Jeremiah,
Griping,
Groaning,
And objecting!

Go out and win the world for Me!

Every single nation!

Make them My disciples,
Teaching them My words,
My impossible commands,
And all that I have planned!

If you think that is ridiculous
And more than you can stand,
Remember what I said
To that rebel Jeremiah:

"First of all
Don't be afraid to fail,
As most men seem to be,
For I am with you.
Yes, I am.
I AM.
I am with you always.

"Stand up and be a man!"

For now you are on call!

On call!

The moment that My words
Begin to swell your mouth
And tremble on your lips,
A kind of mystery is stirred,
Simmering somewhere.

And what you hear
Is not mere sound,
The hollow drum of voices,
But a timid movement in the heart
And in the dormant mind of man.

Your tongue becomes a holy thing,
A vehicle of silent power
Driven by My Word
To make your speech a sacrament,
A happening for life.

Then man to man
And friend to friend
The mystery ignites
As costly words are spoken,
Words like: "I forgive you
And offer you my hope,
Since God forgives us all
And offers us His love."

For that is part of what it means for you
To be on call.

Where the action is,
There the word must be.

Your words.

Your faith.

And this sacrament of speech
Will be administered abroad

With speaking tongues
Like Mine and yours.

And the impossible may then
Be possible
On the tip of tongues like yours —
Touched by God.

part two

A Conversation with Christ

Did You call, Christ?

You did?

From where are You calling?
From the council above?
The mountain?
The Father's house?
The Word?

It doesn't matter where?

No, it doesn't,
I suppose.

But it's hard to hear You,
Sometimes.

Very hard.

You speak with us
As God would speak.
You are the Word of God,
You say.

Okay.

And now You ask us all to speak,
To go and talk of God,
To talk it up,
To live it up,
And change our world.

Seems simple,
So simple.

But it's not!
It's rough.

Like skiing
Or forgiving.

Could You help us
Perhaps?

Could You?

Yes, we'll try,
But—

We're busy too!

Well,
Help us to talk,
To say the words,
To live the talk,
And make our speech
A song,
A sacrament.

A strange word?
But You know what we mean.
Our God alive
Within our words.
Right?

What should we talk about?

Specifically?

All things.

How about You Yourself
And pimples and God
And quivering lips and You,
And eggs and hidden embryos
And fresh blood and You,
And dirty dollars and hair curlers
And guinea pigs and You,
And us
And genes
And grace
And You?

But how?
How much at a time?

And when?

That's not secondary
At all!

Then
Form the word "forgive"

Upon our lips
And between our teeth.

Untie our tongues,
Untangle our minds
To see and say,
"I will forgive,
For God forgives
Others just like me."

To say it
And mean it
And live it.

But that's hard,
So hard to do.

Someone is coming, Lord.
But don't go.

For God's sake,
What shall I say?

"Hi."
"Nice day."

part one

CHAPTER TWO

SiGNS oF THE TiMES

Prophet:
As soon as I became a prophet,
Things began to pop
And jerk
And swing in all directions
From my rooftop.

For God was getting through to me
In almost everything I saw:
In sticks and stones,
In cokes and cones,
And even in a drunkard on the street
About to snore!

I could hear God talking
In the plain
And old
And mundane things I knew.

Wild and unbelievable, I guess,
But true!

Have you ever had your ears cleaned out
And had the muck removed
So that you can hear
As you've never heard before,
And every little whisper
Is a sonic booming cry?
And scratching at a pimple
Is like scraping tin on tin?
And combing through your hair
Is like coming through the rye?

Well,
That's the way it was with me
When I was made alive
To the meaning of the things I saw
That I had never seen before—
Yes, even when I heard a drunkard snore!

At first there was a strong kick,
A victor's thrill,
A crazy happening
That overwhelmed my will.

I would wander down the road,
Kicking at the gravel in disgust,
When suddenly
From at my feet
The Word of God would come to me
In lines that sounded like a childhood song I knew—
And rather foolish too!

"Hey, there, Jerry, what do you see?"

"I see a springy almond rod, Lord."

"No, that's not what it is at all.
That's My strong Word springing into action.
You see?
So it's more than just a springy almond rod
To Me!"

That word kept haunting me
Just like some maddening melody
That will not let you free:

"Hey, there, Jerry, what do you see?"

"I see a pot that's smoking southward."

"No, that's not what it is at all.
That's an evil coming from the northland.
You see?
So it's more than a pot that's smoking southward
To Me!"

The word was there,
Everywhere,
Even on the littered lanes,
Where drunkards snored
Or drank and swore
And screamed at me once more:

"Hey, there, Jerry, what do you say?"

"Every bottle will be filled with wine, sir!"

"No, that's not what is going to happen.
Everybody will be filled with God's wrath.
You see?

So that's more than just some wine in bottles
To me."

I learned to read the signs,
Written, veiled, forgotten,
That God was going into action,
To hurl a vile catastrophe
Like a missile from the north
To devastate His nation
And execute His sputtering wrath
Along a bloody path
Of sin.

I,
I could see it coming,
Gleaming like a black-and-green tornado
Swirling from the eye of God.
It seemed as though I saw
God drinking down His own wrath
Instead of pouring anger forth
From His smoking crimson cup.

Now that fuming cup
Had filled itself again,
And God had had enough.
He summoned me before His court
Cringing!
All His council knew this wasn't any bluff.

"Take this cup of wine," He said,
"This is My cup of wrath,
Which every evil nation on the earth
Must gulp in gallon measure
Until it staggers stupidly
Before the quiver of My face,
Burning with disgrace."

The cup of wrath was red,
For the cup of wrath meant blood,
A rumble at the hand of God,
According to His word,
A bitter, choking word —
Of death.

That evil was an enemy
Racing from the north,
Speeding madly forth

Like some hoodlum on a hot rod,
To zero in on Israel,
Who was slated for disaster
By an angry master.

That deadly ill kept coming,
Penetrating deeper
Until I saw within my mind
Jerusalem besieged
And her glistening heart exposed
To quiver
And shiver in the ash,
Sucking lifeless air
Until she died,
Before what seemed the heartless view of God
On high!

The doom that shattered Israel
Burst into my brain
And tore the minute membrane of my mind
Until I felt insane:

    "My God! My God!
    The pain in my guts
    Is the pain of a twisting sword.
    My God, My God!
    The pang in my breast
    Is the pang of a scorching acid."

I too have tested in advance
What God has long endured:
The wrath that burns when sin abounds
And binds the hands of men!

At last
I saw the wrath descend—
I saw the end.
I gazed upon the earth,
And all the withered world was chaos,
A swirling, putrid chaos,
A putrid, purple chaos,
Just as it had been
Before the world began.
I saw
No man of clay,
No bird of grey,

No pillars for the sky.
No left or right,
No pristine light,
Nothing
But anger from on high,
Black anger from on high,
Black anger,
Black on black on deep purple,
Harboring a cold,
Primeval moan —
All alone!

The end was ugly!

The end was endless.

How I wish that I had never seen
A thing
And never will again!

Kids:
Are you joking Jeremiah?
Are you poking fun at us?
God doesn't talk in silly signs
Like that!

It doesn't really work
When I listen to the blackbirds
Or the bees
To learn about the facts of life
From God,
Of God,
And what on earth He's doing.

We cannot hear some secret voice
Peeping in our ears
When we see a snoring drunkard
Or some French bread on the table
Or we watch a barbecue
Blowing pungent fumes of steak
Across the neighbor's well-mown yard —
And another barbecue.

What we hear
Is like a fear
That all of this won't last.

And that is hardly God,
Hardly anything!

So sing your song for us!
Sing it, Uncle Jerry.
We hope you don't object
If we start to call you uncle —
And sing along with you:

   "Hey, there, Jerry, what do you see?"

     "Every bottle will be filled with wine, sir."

   "No, that's not what is going to happen.
   Everybody will be filled with God's wrath.
   You see?
   So that's more than just some wine in bottles
   To me!"

Your songs are very clever, Jeremiah,
But do you really mean
That God would fill His people up with wrath
And make them drunk
With bloody, cold disaster?

God is Love,
And, heavens above,
He wouldn't do a thing like that!
Just like that!

God doesn't wrap the world in wrath
Or some eerie cloak of death
Till all of life is chilled and blue,
Gasping for a stolen breath.

Why should God use aimless evil nations
As His sacred front,
A clumsy camouflage
For the war against His own kind,
The people that He loved
But who didn't understand?

And we don't understand
What kind of God
Would use a rod
To whip the world
And make it reel
From head to heel
Before it's hurled
Into eternity!

If we must see black signs like these,
Or talk about red wrath
That cups of curious wine provoke,
We rather skip the whole affair
And go and have a coke.

The Lord:
I hope you're not offended
If I interrupt again
Before you have a coke.
What Jeremiah said
Was really not a joke!

40

I'd like to have you walk with Me,
To watch with Me
For just an hour or two
In a garden called Gethsemane,
Where I have been before,
And felt God's wrath descend.

Can you hate a Man in agony,
A Man about to die,
A Man who throws His voice
In a frantic, muffled cry?

"My Father, My Father,
Is there just a chance
That I don't need
To drink this cup of Mine,
Or is that out of line?

"Just as You say!
Your will be done —
Your way!"

His cup of wrath was red,
For His cup of wrath meant death,
The accumulated impact
Of accelerating evil
That finally is spent
In the suffering Son of God.

For sin is not a black mark in a book,
Or simply breaking rules,
But harmful forces
You have set in motion
When you disobey your God
Or break up with your friends
And hurt the guys you like.

And so I beg of you,
Please heal that injury
Before a greater wrong is done.
That's why I'd like to have you eat with Me,
To drink with Me,
For just an hour or two
In the upper room
Where I have been before
And felt God's love descend.

Can you hear a Man in agony,
A Man about to die,
A Man who is speaking now
Across the table where you sit?

Take and eat,
For this is more than bread you see.
This is My own body,
Which is given up to misery.

Take and drink.
This is more than wine you see.
This is My own blood that has been shed
And poured into this cup.
Because I drank the cup of wrath,
I drank it in your stead,
And the cup was crimson red.

When you take that cup from Me,
Its power is now reversed,
The wrath is spent
And forgiveness set in motion,
A powerful word from God
To heal and help
And vitalize —
Rebel girls and guys.

When God gets through to you
In the sacrament of bread and wine
In some cool, uncanny way,
Then they should be a sign
As sharp as any Jeremiah saw
That God is still at work today
And that I will come again
To dine with you
And offer you
A vision of tomorrow.

And should you see a war
Or two men fighting on the street,
Remember, they are signs
That I am coming as a judge
To set all matters straight.

But should you see two men shake hands in Christ
Or a man and woman reconciled,

Forgiving one another without reservation,
Remember, that's a sign
That I have brought you back to God
To heal your broken ties with men
And forgive the wrongs you've done to Him.

For now, through Me,
Every cup of wine or coke
May be a kind of sacrament,
A stimulant of faith
That God was there
And you are here
Entirely by His grace.

he
took
the cup
of
wrath
and
drained
it
to the
dregs

WITH CUP IN HAND

Spokesman:
The Lord be with you,
    with you and within you,
    with you in your pious fears,
    with you in your twisted doubt,
    with you as you worship,
        as you dream and dance and shout.
May the Lord get through to you!

Kids:
And to your spirit too!

Spokesman:
Lift up your hearts,
    your heads and unsealed lips,
    your songs and wild new beat,
    your fresh potato chips,
    your swinging, shuffling feet,
        swinging back to Christ!
Lift your lives from laziness!

Kids:
We lift them to the Lord.

Spokesman:
Let us give thanks unto the Lord our God,
    thanks for life and love,
    thanks for what we are,
    thanks for what Christ is,
    thanks for coins and car,
    thanks for hope that's on the way,
        for fresh forgiveness every day!

Let us give thanks!

Kids:
It's meet and right so to do!
Yes, indeed,
that is the least that we can do!

Spokesman:
It's truly meet and right and salutary,
which means in fact
that God is liberating you
    from you yourselves,
    from getting mad at what you are,

and getting miserable inside
because you cannot make the grade
or hit the spot
or find the slot
or be on top
flying with excitement
all the time!

Kids:
Yes, God our Father
sets our spirits free
when all the time
and everywhere
with silent thoughts
we are aware
that He is there
creating life in life
and love for life
in all the world
for me
and every struggling tree!

Spokesman:
So then we do not sit alone,
sweat alone,
sing alone,
fret alone.

Kids:
We join with every being
everywhere,
every force
and every will
upon the earth
and in the air,
to hail our Lord,
to celebrate His day,
to laud and magnify,
to praise His glorious name
and say:

Spokesman:
Holy! Holy! Holy!
Lord God of Hosts.

Kids:
Power! Power! Power!
The limit and the greatest!
The King above all powers.
A God who is unique!

Spokesman:
Heaven and earth
are full of Thy glory.

Kids:
Universe and atom
responding to Your power,
full of life!

Spokesman:
Hosanna! Hosanna!
Hosanna in the highest.

Kids:
Praise Him! Cheer Him!
Praise for all you're worth!

Spokesman:
Blessed is He,
blessed is He,
blessed is He that cometh
in the name of the Lord.

Spokesman:
He is more than mighty;
He is more than great;
He is more than some big name;
He comes as Christ the Lord,
but He's coming just the same!

Hosanna! Hosanna!
Hosanna in the highest.

Kids:
Praise Him! Cheer Him!
Praise for all you're worth!

Spokesman:
Our Father who art in heaven,
Hallowed be Thy name;
Thy kingdom come;
Thy will be done on earth as it is in heaven;
Give us this day our daily bread;
And forgive us our trespasses
As we forgive those who trespass against us;
And lead us not into temptation;
But deliver us from evil;

Kids:
For Thine is the kingdom
and the power and the glory
forever and ever. Amen.

Spokesman:
Amen! Amen!

Kids:
Amen! Amen!
Let's say it again.

For You have control,
and You have the power,
spectacular power,
supreme in its scope —
and there is our hope
as long as we live.

Spokesman:
Our Lord Jesus Christ,
the night He was betrayed,
took bread,
and after giving thanks
He broke the bread
and gave to His disciples,
saying:

Take and eat.
This is My body
given for you;
this do
in remembrance of Me.

Kids:
Betrayed by friend
and almost dead,
He still gave thanks
and broke the bread
as others broke His body.

Yet through that bread
    our Lord got through;
    that God was real
    and His body too
    in a strange and sacred way
    that still holds true.

Spokesman:
In much the same way
He took the cup
after supper,
returned thanks,
and gave it to them,
saying:

    Take and drink.
    This cup's the new covenant
    in My blood,
    shed for you
    for the forgiveness of sins.
    This do,
    whenever you drink it,
    in remembrance of Me.

Kids:
He took the cup of wrath,
    our red cup of death,
    and drained it to the dregs,
    until His blood came pouring forth
    in death.
He drained our cup of wrath
    until His broken veins
    poured blood
    into this cup of life
    as a cup of rich forgiveness
    offered here
    each time we drink
    with cup in hand

remembering His pain
and His victory for us.

Spokesman:
The peace of the Lord be with you always.
A peace that means assurance
    that in our frantic racing
    through a million anxious hours
    we have a bond
    that cannot break,
    for God Himself
    has tied the cords
    of faith and life
    on either end.

Kids:
Amen again!

We cannot quite explain it,
    and we cannot really feel it.
    But yet we know somehow
    that in some way
    we can be sure of God,
    who is bigger than us all.

The sign of the times
is still the sign of the cross.

Spokesman:
O Christ, Thou Lamb of God,
that takest away the sin of the world,

Kids:
Have mercy upon us.
Take a fresh look at us.
Get a good hold of us.
Once more accept from us
whatever we happen to be.

Spokesman:
O Christ, Thou Lamb of God,
that takes away the sin of the world,

Kids:
Have mercy upon us.
Take a fresh look at us.
Get a good hold of us.

Once more accept from us
whatever we happen to be.

Spokesman:
O Christ, Thou Lamb of God,
that takest away the sin of the world,

Kids:
Grant us Thy peace
to face what it means
as sinners abroad
who speak of a God
that the public ignores
but our faith still acclaims!

Spokesman:
Amen.

Kids:
Amen and then
With cup in hand
Amen again.

part one

CHAPTER THREE

SUCH ANTICS

Prophet:
I've just been down to the local square
To buy down there
A long, white, linen undershirt
Free from dirt,
A normal thing to do, I guess.

Well, that was "in" for us
To wear shirts thus
Underneath our hairy robes.

I wore the thing for weeks and weeks
Until the cloth was dirty,
Absolutely filthy.
And that was "in" for God,
Which you may think is odd,
But I didn't take it off
Until He gave the word.

And
When I did, it stank!
The thing was rank.

And God, who couldn't stand it anymore,
Shouted through my door:

"Take that putrid rag
And bury it four hundred miles from here
Beside a rumbling river
In the land of Babylon,
Where all My dying people soon must go,
Shackled hand to hand,
A sloppy band
Of exiles,
Slaves, and
Whores."

I anchored down my moldy shirt
Behind an old, wet rock
And staggered home relieved,
Or so I thought
Until my mind was caught
By God's relentless pitch.

"Return," He said,
"Oh, no," said I!

"Oh, yes," He said.
"Oh, well!" said I
And traveled back again
400 heavy miles.

I found that cloth
Like flesh decayed and damp,
Smelling like the meat
That ravenous dogs
Will drag along the street.

I held that shirt aloft
As though it were
An umpire's checkered flag.
And the latest word of God came through
Like the smell that reached
The naked nostrils
Of all who wandered by.

"Look at yourselves," says God,
"And see yourselves as I do.
Your putrid yellow pride
Will bring you black corruption,
For I will let you rot
In a damp and dirty land
Until you're good for nothing,
Nothing but the garbage dump!

"That's quite a slump!

"Long ago
I made you cling to Me
Like a fragrant, linen undershirt,
Close and fresh and clean.

"With a covenant
I bound you to My loins,
A dancing bride
Too shy to show her shining face.

"But now!
You have a harlot's brow.

"Every day you wear a mask,
A mask for kissing wooden calves,
A mask for petting pagan kings,

A mask for spitting on the poor,
A mask for praying on the floor
Of My temple,
Of My slum.

"I will tell you, My beloved,
What you are:
A mutilated mask
Pocked with sin
Which cannot be erased.
Your mask, you see,
Became your skin!
And just as leopards
Cannot change their spots,
You cannot change your lives
Dark with evil blots
Breaking through your flesh!

"The ugly mask you wore
Is precisely what you are—
Rotten to the core."

There are sweeter jobs, I'm sure,
Than waving rotten rags about
And rubbing dirty noses
Until their nerves are raw.

Can you see *this earthen flask*
With its long and naked neck
Like that of a soft and slender girl,
A tender girl
Untouched by lusting lips?

This flask belongs to God,
A sacred flask selected
For display,
Not for play!

This flask belongs to God!
It is the people of God
Formed by God to love,
To demonstrate His glory
And reflect His face.

You see this flask?
I take it now

And dash it on a stone
The way some kids
Throw bottles on the street
When they are all alone
And want to vent their spleen.

You cannot mend that flask,
And that's the way it's meant to be,
For God is on the track,
In racing gear,
Set to run His people down
And break them into pieces,
Worthless pieces,
Junkyard pieces!

Can you see *this yoke,*
A wooden yoke around my neck?
I wear it for the curious crowd
To make them all aware
That God will force them all to share
The yoke of slavery to Babylon
No matter what they plan.

I wear a yoke,
I break a flask,
I wear a dirty undershirt!
If you ask
Just why I do these acts for God,
Remember that I'm called to be
The Word of God alive.
I live His waiting wrath,
I show His doom
By all my ugly antics.

I have no wife,
I have no kids,
I do not even sing and dance
With any of my people,
For I am living out each day
The fact that God is now alone,
A loving God
Deserted by His own,
Rejected by His sons,
Unwanted and unknown.

For every act
Is more than just a symbol.
It is the Word made visible
Working through my actions
To bring about the end
They must vividly portray —

That final day for Israel.
Such antics are the Word of God!

So, if you want to save your skin
And see disaster through,
Then turn your face to God
And surrender to the enemy,
To pagan Babylon,
And pray on his behalf!
That's the only thing to do!

Kids:
Are you fooling, Jeremiah?
Are you laughing up your sleeve?
God doesn't play the fool with kids,
With kids like us, like that.

He doesn't make them do
Such wild repulsive stunts.
He doesn't make us act like that,
Like nutty circus runts.

59

Your kind of preaching, Jeremiah,
Is really rather vile,
For we are far too civilized
To worship bulls
Or something out of style.

What would they say?
Yes, what would our people say,
If our poor old preacher walked in one day
With a beartrap round his neck
Or a bowl upon his head?
Yes, what would they say?

Can you hear him now
As he beats some sacred cow:

All you women will be broken
Just the way I break this bowl,
Because you worry more about your head,
About your plastered face
And frizzed-up, spray-set hair,
Than you do about your God!

And all the men who try to live
As though there is no meaning
Or no sin in life
Will soon be caught
Beneath their chin
As the evil they have done
Crawls up and closes in!

What would they say?
Yes, what would our pious people say
If we held a demonstration in the church
Or a "sit in" down the aisles?
Yes, what would they say?

What would they do
If we wore green masks
Depicting two-faced people
Who say that worship is the thing
But never give a rap
About the dying and the lonely,
About the starving or insane,
About the wasteful wars we fight,
Or the slaughter in our streets?

We see the sham of adult men
Whispering their prayers
To gain a higher income,
And guzzling down their beers
But never really brooding
About the day our world will burn
In violent nuclear flame
As white atomic missiles
Strike
At friend and foe alike.

Some men within the church
Seem satisfied to smile
At the face they see
Reflected from the altar.
But when they turn away,
Their faith is blind
To the death and dope
That lurk behind.

What would they say?
Yes, what would our phony people say
If we interrupted any pastor
By screaming from the choir loft
That people in our prisons
Were freer than so many
Trapped inside the church,
Who dribble selfish prayers
Instead of bringing strength
To bitter prisoners everywhere?
Yes, what would they say?

They say the church is where we live,
That we can do within His house
All that we would do before our God at home.
But that simply isn't true —
At least not in the churches
Where most of us were taught.

What would they say?
Yes, what would our people say
If we were asked to choose for God
In a final nuclear war?
What would happen to our faith
If God would send an enemy
To wipe us from the globe
In one great cosmic blast?

Would we surrender to the foe
For the sake of Christ our Lord
If we thought we heard God telling us
To bring forgiveness,
The Gospel of our God,
To that foe?

Could we suffer for our Lord
If the doom of God
Descended from the skies
In a pink-and-orange mushroom cloud
Of death?

Are you fooling, Jeremiah?
Are you making fools of us?
God doesn't make His wishes clear
To kids like us, like that.

He doesn't tell us all:
"Surrender to the foe,"
And make us look like traitors, then,
Before each pious Joe.

Your kind of antics, Jeremiah,
Still make us rather ill.
You just can't tell the teen-age crowd
To yell aloud: "Surrender, men, at will!"

The Lord:
May I speak a word with you,
Young men,
Impatient men and glib,
Scoffing at the word
Of younger men of yesterday?
May I speak a word, I say?

63

May I speak it with a yoke?
With a flask or with a shirt
As Jeremiah did?

May I say it with a whip
As I tip
The bargain tables
Crackling with coins
Across the pitted temple floor
Among the beggars and the flops?
I hardly need to add
That the house of God our Lord
Should never be
A gutted den of hoodlums
Or of cops.
Perhaps I ought to speak
With a hot patrolman's stick
As I watch you pick
Your way
Where festering green gangs
Are ready to explode
And mutilate your gleaming flesh,
Your eyes,
Your altars —
And then you'd understand, young man,
Or would you?

May I say a word?
May I say it by a bed
On which a Jewish boy is paralyzed,
Drained,
Almost dead?
May I say, "Take heart, My boy,
For I forgive your sins"?
Or are those ancient, empty words?
Then may I say,
"Take up your bed,
And carry it back home"?
And may I ask your youthful pleasure
As you see that boy
Return with joy
Jumping on his bed?
Perhaps I ought to speak
With a doctor's stethoscope
And scalpel
As you watch your father dying,

Mugged by creeps.
And then you'd understand,
Young man,
Or would you?

May I speak another word?
May I say it with some water
As a frantic prophet pours it slowly
On My head
And God's Spirit from above
Invades My life
To move Me into action?
Will you let God speak from heaven
To tell you who I am?
Will you have Him part the clouds
And designate His chosen Son?
No sooner said than done?
But perhaps I ought to speak
With vitamins and pills
Or bands that beat and swing
With a spirit
And a sting
That sends you into orbit —
And then you'd understand,
Young man!
Or would you?

I do not need to spell out
Word by word
The point of all My acts.
For all I did
Was Word —
The final Word — from God.
I am the Word,
A word that you can see,
You see.
I bring alive
That strange, mysterious depth
Called God.
In Me you can observe
The source of life brought to the surface.
In Me you see the face,
The unseen face,
The silent Word
First spoken at creation,
Now exposed to view.

That's why I ask you all
To take a little water
And believe Me when I say,
"Your sins are all forgiven."
For the Spirit enters in
To rouse My leaping word
And make anew
That which is you.

Yes, take a little water
When you dine and when you bathe,
When you kiss and when you plant,
When you bring your child to Me,
And the water with My Word
Will lift your life
From first to third,
Where God will drive you home.

part two

Reliving Our Baptism

how can drops of water transfer you to the grave of a man who died long centuries ago?

iNTo THe WATeR

Spokesman:
In the name of the Father
And of the Son
And of the Holy Spirit.

Kids:
Amen.

Spokesman:
Well, now, what do you want?

Kids:
We come with water
And with word in hand.

Spokesman:
I do not understand.

Kids:
We wish to live anew
What God can do
When men baptize
And open searching eyes
To Christ our Lord.

Spokesman:
As infants you were blessed.
The ritual is through!

Kids:
Precisely, man, precisely!
And you said it very nicely.
But we wish to trace again
What happened to us then.

Spokesman:
But you are growing men!

Kids:
Precisely, man, precisely!
That's why we wish to know exactly
What it means.

Spokesman:
From where do you come?

Kids:
We come from many corners
Of the twentieth century!
From a subdivision
With police escorting us,
Down a wide divided highway
With our safety belts attached,
Through a curling clover leaf
And within a safety zone,
From the IBM computers
With insurance to the hilt!

Spokesman:
But how do you come,
You by yourselves?

Kids:
We come as men,
Like other growing men,
Miserable and mortal men,
Addicts, ill, and alcoholics,
Neurotics, torn by sex,
Boys frustrated by delay,
Crying women cold,
No more adored,
Lonely kids together
And sick, sick, sick!

Spokesman:
You're not as bad as that.
I know you kids myself.

Kids:
We come as one of them,
Morbid men,
Belonging to a race of rebels
Like Cain and Cleopatra,
Like mother and like father.

Spokesman:
Is there nothing you can bring
To preserve your dignity?

Kids:
We come as men
Living in God's image,

Regents on His globe,
But we fall,
We flirt,
We probe,
We doubt,
We squeal,
We probe,
And we find
That we are dust!

Spokesman:
To whom do you come
As men from the ground?

Kids:
To One who is one of us!
To Him who lived with men.
With crude old prostitutes,
With beggars cruder still,
With snotty kids and kooks,
With addicts who were ill,
With anyone and everyone
Who needed help and hope.

Spokesman:
And who is this
Who does all this?

Kids:
A man called Jesus Christ
Who spoke the Word of God
To come and be forgiven
With water
And the power of God from heaven.

Spokesman:
How can He help you now
With water and with words?

Kids:
We come to follow Him,
Take up His cross and follow Him,
Behold that Man and die with Him,
Pass through His gloomy grave
By passing through the water
And come to live with Him,

To eat and dance with Him
As soon as we are dry.

Spokesman:
How can drops of water
Transfer you to the grave
Of a man who died
Long centuries ago?

Kids:
We don't know
For sure.
But the Word of God
Is more
Than just a sound.
We believe
That Christ is still alive,
And when we come to Him,
We join Him
So that all He is we are.
Just as we live like men
By birth in blood and water,
So now we live in Christ
By birth in Word and water.

Spokesman:
Your logic isn't sound.
We are not born again.

Kids:
We speak from faith,
The faith of little kids,
For logic cannot answer
The meaning and the depth
Of life.

Spokesman:
Who can?

Kids:
Jesus Christ,
The One who gave us life
With a little water
And His word!

Spokesman:
I heard!

And I hear it now once more:
"Young men, I baptize you
In the name of Father, Son,
And of the Holy Spirit."

Kids:
Amen, Amen.
Let's say it when we're swimming
Or when it rains again.
Let's say it when we shower
And relive our faith as men.

Spokesman:
Amen! Young men!
Amen!

part one

CHAPTER FOUR

HANG DOWN YOUR HEAD JEREMIAH

Prophet:
I wrote a private diary
With all the gripes
And all the guff
Which I could fling
To make it rough
On God
For all He did to me—
Or rather,
All He didn't do!

My sweaty prayers
May turn you off
Or turn you on—who knows?

I wrote them
On the cutting edge of suicide,
The outer point of sanity,
Beside the grave.

If you want to play
The part of God along the way,
Your snapping souls
May find a kindred spirit
In His sharp replies—
That's if you like
To throw mud pies.

Here my sweaty prayers begin:

Listen here, God!

Listen here, God.
There's a limit to the slime
That a normal man can take
When it's rubbed into his face!

I've had nothing else but snarls
Since You hypnotized my lips
With Your itchy words,
Your biting words,
Your crackling words
That make me clench my mouth,
Tighten up my chest,
And sob!

I'm an addict to Your Word
That dribbles through my teeth.
I cannot kick it back!
O God,
Why won't You let me lose
This hideous preaching habit,
This yoke across my jaw?

Kids:
You have no right to talk like that,
Like a serpent with an ulcer!
God formed you with His fingertips
Inside your mother's womb.
He picked you
And appointed you,
He checked you out,
Anointed you,
And classified you as a prophet
Fit for duty.

He gave you His own promise,
And He gave you His own words
As if you were His son.
What more can you possibly want,
Jeremiah?
What more?

> *Hang down your head, Jeremiah!*
> *Hang down your head and cry:*
> *"Why was I born a prophet?*
> *Please, God, please tell me why!"*

Prophet:
The sniveling, God!

What about their drivel, God?
The whispering,
The snickering,
The gargling
And bickering
That pound against my brain?

I prayed for all those people
On my knees,
On my face,
On their sidewalks

And their coffins
If you please.

They heard my cry,
And so did God,
But they kicked me in the back
To watch me wince
And die.

Do You enjoy their sport, Lord God?
Their pious game,
Their dirty thrills
At my expense!

O God,
Why can't You understand?
Why must You be so dense?

I'm innocent!
I'm clean!
I haven't cursed,
I haven't lied,
I haven't damned,
Or even worse, blasphemed.

Test me, God, and see!

Then why am I in pain?

Just tell me that!

Other men can get away
With things that bring me grief.
Other men, like punks and snobs,
Can live a life of peace.
Other men can tear a woman
And calmly leave her lie.
Other men can beat a child,
And others won't ask why.

Why, You righteous God? Why?

Kids:
Poor prophet!

Do you think this round was rough,
Rough enough to make you spit?

Do you wish a tender pat
To make you feel accepted?
Do you long for heavenly pity
Because you're sorry for yourself?
Do you think it's hard to keep the pace
With the infantry of Israel?

Do you, prophet?

Then wait until you face the cavalry
And sprint to save your life.
And wait until you see the jungles,
Where very few survive.
And wait until you feel the cruelty
Of carrying God's cross.
And wait until you taste a traitor's death
Before you scream for blood.

Hang loose, prophet!

> *Hang down your head, Jeremiah!*
> *Hang down your head and cry:*
> *"Give me a taste of freedom!*
> *Teach me the way to die!"*

Prophet:
What is freedom, God?

Free?

What is freedom, God,
When Your words in my mouth
Are like screams in my soul,
Burning my bowels,
Grinding my bones,
Inflaming my liver,
And forcing a taste of bile to my lips?

I hate this taste of bile!
I hate this word of death.
I hate Your song of anger,
And I hate the way You mock me, God,
Underneath Your breath.

For every time I try
To shut my mouth
Or hold my tongue
Or clench my fist

77

Or bite my lip
Or close my eyes to what is going on,
A sudden urge comes over me,
A violent spasm smashes me,
And I am forced to shout,
To violently insist
That God is God!

I am forced to say God's anger
Is an evil, active storm
Hovering above,
Sputtering on the fringe,
Waiting for the word from God
To buckle, break, and burst
Upon our heads.

My lip is bleeding, Lord.

Please get it over with.
Please turn Your storm
Toward my foes,
And bring Your vengeance down,
Before I lose my mind!

Kids:
God is with you!
That's the line:

> "I am with you to protect you,
> To fortify and build you,
> To deliver and exalt you,
> To satisfy and praise you!"

Don't you remember?

You have the secrets
From the council in the sky,
And you have no cause
To modify the beauty,
The glory of God's wrath
Upon His pagan people.

Rejoice in what you preach,
And do not knock it, man.
For God the Lord is on your side!
And that's the way to go

If you really want to know.
Or should we ask the enemy
If God loves Uncle Sam?

But you love it,
Don't you, Jeremiah?
You're a ham, a real ham!

Now aren't you, Jeremiah?

> *Hang down your head, Jeremiah!*
> *Hang down your head and cry:*
> *"Where is Your bloody vengeance?*
> *Where is my victory?"*

Prophet:
A shimmering mirage!

All I see is grief, God,
Grief and bleeding pain
Flowing through the fallow fields,
The streets, the ruts,
The temple and its stones.

You can tolerate
The kind of vicious evils,
The livid, lurid ills,
That propagate across the land
And in the sea
And everywhere I turn
Like whims of fate
That flit across my path!

Can You, God?

You can let a child be born
And let his mind be twisted,
Turned by jagged wheels
Into a snorting beast,

Can You?

You can cross a path
And hear a woman murdered in Your wake
And never look behind
And stop the bleeding or the rape,

Can You?

God, You know You have seduced me,
Seized and overpowered me
As if I were a virgin in the fields,
Waiting for Your promise of protection
From the beasts.

No matter how I look at it,
God deceives His men!
He has the power
And the opportunity
To interrupt at any time
Instead of calmly watching,
Watching through the dirty panes
Of a second-story window
As the prisoners below
Stumble down the road.

I come to Him for healing on the way,
I stop beside Him for refreshment
As I would beside a friendly brook,
But I find the spring of life is dry.

He is like sweet, shining water in the distance
That promises new life
But vanishes like quicksilver
Or a shimmering mirage,
A shimmering mirage
Which doesn't keep its word.

You heard, God!

Kids:
You cannot get away with that!

You've gone too far
With all your bold demands
Before the throne of God!

In fact,
You've lost your job
Unless you'll first admit
That God's in charge
And what He says
Is something well worth saying
No matter how you feel,
No matter what you think,
No matter what that means
For struggling men of God.

Is that clear?

Do you think God wants to hear
Every puny doubt
Or every bit of sweaty prayer
That gushes from your soul?

Do you?

Is God really quite that interested
In all the dirt and lust of life
That seem to haunt your heart?

Is He, sir?

Surely God has better things to do
Than wander through the seamy streets
And search for evil holes to fill.

Well, hasn't He?

Ask a girl like Mary Magdalene
As she washes Jesus' feet.

> *Hang down your head, Jeremiah!*
> *Hang down your head and cry:*
> *"Why was I born to suffer,*
> *Why won't You let me die?"*

Prophet:
Why was I born at all?

Why was I born at all
If all my life is woe,
If all I find is misery,
If all I ask is brushed aside
By a brusk and brutal God?

Why was I born at all
If everything I've learned
Is challenged by experience
And nothing stands the test
When life gets underway?

Why was I born at all
If death is all I need

To find relief from blood and hate,
From raw discipleship,
From suffering without hope?

Why was I born at all
If God will never prove
That He is really God
And not a bleary idol
Who cannot see the sky?

Why was I born at all
If I can't be myself
And force my deepest doubts
Before the face of God?

Why, God, why?

Why won't You answer me?

God!

One word?

Any word!

God! God! God!

Kids:
Hang down your head, Jeremiah!
Hang down your head and cry:
"Why is there no tomorrow?
Why was I born? Oh, why?"

The Lord:
I'd like to have you listen
To some things I've said before
About your life of suffering
With thorns and wood
And flying rocks,
With tears and salt
And matted hair,
With cans and glass
And angry cops,
With snorts and jeers
That crack the air.

I send you out
As sheep in the midst of wolves.
So be as wise as serpents are
And as innocent as doves.
Beware of men you meet,
For they'll take you into court
And flog you in their schools,
And they will drag you out
Before governors and heads
For My sake
To testify to them
And to the world at large.

84

And when they get a hold on you,
Don't be anxious
How you ought to speak
Or what you ought to say,
For what you have to say
Will come to you right then!
You aren't the one, you see,
Who does the real talking,
But the Spirit of your Father,
Who is talking in and through you.

Brother will deliver brother to death,
And the father his own child;
Children will rise against parents
And have them put to death;
And you —
You will be hated by all
For the sake of My name.
But the man who takes it all
Down to the bitter end
Will be free.

Your tears and pain
Can be a sacrament of love:
Living in the shoes of others,
Sitting in and screaming out,
Before Me and with Me,
Because of Me and with Me,
In spite of Me and with Me
To the end.

And when you taste My tears
The way that Jeremiah has,
You'll know the need
For more than puffy tissues
To pacify your eyes
And prayers.

You'll know the reason why
You heard a dying Prophet cry:
"Why hast Thou forsaken Me, My God,
Oh, why?"

And He will help you live
Through the special power of suffering
Before you die.

a cup
of
COLD
Water

part two

*A Litany for Those
Who Get Involved*

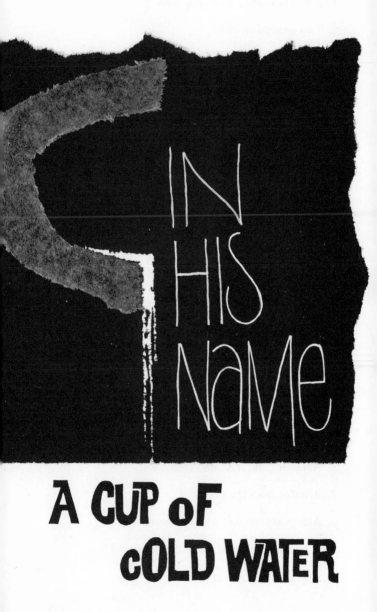

IN HIS NAME

A CUP oF cOLD WATER

1. A cup of cold water.

2. A cup of cold water in His name.

1. A cup of black coffee or a coke.

2. Two aspirin or more.

1. A cigaret, a match, a deep breath.

2. A dollar in the gutter.

1. A fall, a scramble, and a sudden smile.

2. A bottle for a while.

1. Sunshine splattered on the wall.

2. A green shoot on the pavement.

1. A fire hydrant and a kid.

2. Another kid, a pair of dirty trunks.

1. A screaming car, a groan.

2. A pair of dying punks.

1. A cup of cold water.

2. A cup of cold water in His name.

1. A greeting and a curse – or worse.

2. A word about the weather.

1. A shrug, a smile, a missing tooth.

2. Another cigaret, a stop sign.

1. A letter from the past.

2. A drunken mother and a dream.

1. A scattered newspaper and a crumpled bag.

2. A sandwich and a crust.

1. A cup of cold water.

2. A cup of cold water in His name.

1. A passing taxicab, a lump of gum.

2. A familiar scent of perfume in the air.

1. A pair of legs, a pair of poodles.

2. A tip, a heavy bag, a swinging door.

1. A blaring radio, a cool beat.

2. A cop beside the car.

1. A shot, a scream, a passing dog.

2. A priest, a prayer, another cop.

1. A little girl, a little doll.

2. A little baby's bottle.

1. A cup of cold water.

2. A cup of cold water in His name.

1. A question and a question mark.

2. A smeared window and a pain.

1. A search without success.

2. A pretty face, a torn dress, a slip.

1. A bandage and a pin.

2. A heap of words, a heavy noise.

1. A sigh, a shock, a broken mirror.

2. A ringside seat, a withered hand.

1. A pair of shoes, an empty sky.

2. A touch of blood.

1. Two planks of wood.

2. A stretcher and a hill.

1. A needle and a drug.

2. Some vinegar and wine.

1. A handkerchief, a dripping sponge, a razor blade.

2. A prayer, a gasp, another cop.

1. A coat, a pair of dirty dice.

2. A lightning flash, a roll of thunder.

1. A haze above, a husky voice.

2. A silent night.

1. A broken leg, a knife wound.

2. A jail, a three-day stay, a sleep.

1. A hangover, a bunch of keys.

2. Another day, another door, a wild, excited yell.

1. A dry throat.

2. A dusty throat.

1. A cup of cold water.

2. A cup of cold water in His name.

1. A cup of cold water.

2. A cup of cold water to his lips.

part one

CHAPTER FIVE

LET's CELEBRATE

Prophet:
I sat alone in prison,
A man of skin and bone in prison,
Alone,
At home in prison now.

I sat alone in prison,
A traitor, so they sneered,
A dog,
A fink,
A rat
Because I dared to take the one risk
Calculated in the end
To save at least the city
As God carried out His plot
To punish all His family
With the swords of maniacs and men.

"Surrender!" was my sermon.
"Give in! Give in!" I cried.
"It doesn't mean you're chicken.
If you try to save your hide!"

But none could understand
How a persecuted prophet
Could urge such cold, hard cowardice
Before a blustering enemy,
A brutal foe,
A Babylonian army.

I sat alone in prison,
Skin and bone in prison,
Unable there to pray.

I felt like any brooding kid
Whose heart is smashed by friends
When all the guys that he respected
Drop him
Like a mongrel dog beside the road,
Disliked,
Disgraced,
Rejected,
And left to wander down the clamoring street
Crying sobs of bile within his stomach,
Stewing stupid thoughts within his head,

Waiting for the one real word: "Come on,"
Which means,
"You are accepted, man!"

And yet
I couldn't pray for them
Since God forbade my sympathy,
My timid intercession,
Until the words I cried
Rose up and died
As stillborn sighs.

It's vicious
When a prophet cannot pray.
Do you understand,
Young men?

I sat alone in prison,
Skin and bone in prison,
And I slowly starved to death,
Breath by brittle breath,
As the screeching, laughing,
Snorting, barking,
Roaring, rumbling,
Gurgling, lumbering army
Encircled the sacred city of Jerusalem
And waited for our husky cry
For mercy,
For water,
And for bread!

But sad to say,
The people of God were tough,
And God let them sweat it out
For three long years
In sick Jerusalem
Before He opened up her heart
To let the trampling messengers of death
Break her heaving walls.

I sat alone in prison
Like the girl who lives next door
Watching as the party of her friend
Spins wildly through the night —
Wishing she were there

And knowing that the whole affair
Was her idea.

I sat alone in prison,
Breath and bone in prison
For months and months on end
Until one day I had a hunch.
I had the faintest feeling
That my cousin,
A rather crafty fellow,
Who thinks I'm dense,
Would offer me his father's land
And try to make me buy
Even though the land
Would soon be in the hands
Of the Babylonian army
And so quite worthless.

I had this hunch, you see,
But when my cousin actually came,
I was very much surprised,
For my hunch, it seems, turned out to be
The very word of God for me!
And so
I bought the land!

Well, no,
My cousin didn't fool me
Although he thought he had,
For God was coming through to me
Loud and clear again
Even though I was alone,
Drying skin and bone,
In prison.

"Your purchase is a sign," said God,
"My guarantee that one new day
I will give My broken people
All this bleeding land again
Where they can buy and sell
And play and scream
And leap and yell
In a land of milk and honey,
Hot-dog stands,
And soft ice cream."

I sat alone and dazed
Like the driver of a speeding car
Who survives a splintering crash
Through the window of a store.
I sat alone and rigid
As the ashes fell around me,
As the land of God was scorched
And the temple crackled like a box,
Where many people thought
Their God had once been caught.

The lost volcanic words
That once I spoke so fiercely
Were coming true before my face —
And how I wish they weren't —
As blood was spilled
And hair was burned.

A puff of ash,
A whisp of dust,
A swirling wind across the cinders
Blurred my vision,
A bloodshot vision
Of God in pain
Struggling with the dust
Again.

I could see a glimmer of tomorrow,
An image of God's new man
Sculptured out of molten dust,
A hot and modern piece of art
That would force the sour adult
To start
And say, "My God, what's that?"

Now I see this new man bound to God
By an endless natal cord
He calls His covenant,
That bond of blood which He has formed
To join His love
To the very source of life.

I see this new man, free and bold,
Leaping, dancing with his God,
Beating out a rhythm,
Swinging with his God,

Flying with the wind
And cool!

I see him take a laughing girl
And fling her in the air,
I see him catch her in his arms
To hold her close
And gently kiss her hair.

I watched and waited.
Will this fresh new man,
Who knows the fierce spirit of life
That God implants within,
Now turn from God
And sin?

This man knew the will of God,
That free and furious drive
To live for God
Because God lives inside,
Forgives inside,
Even when we take Him for a ride.

This man knew his God
As you and I know
All the features of our face.
This man talked to God
As if He were a man,
Another kid
Who understood,
A guy who knew
Just what to do
In any situation.

I watched
To see
If this new man
Would take this girl
And selfishly use her
Or forcefully abuse her
As some guys want to do.

I heard God whisper
To that newborn man,
"You will not harm this girl
Or push her all the way,

For I went all the way to death,
Used by men,
Abused by men,
To show how My forgiveness works
As it suffers,
Strains, and struggles
For the person who is loved,
In the people I forgive.

"Forgiveness is the power,
And forgiveness the arena
For the lives of perfect men
Who are bound to Me by love
In My strong, new covenant,
In this furious dance called life,
Where I never let you go
As My hand clenches yours."

I was alone in prison,
Leaping skin and bone in prison,
Very free in prison,
That day!

"Let's celebrate,"
I heard God say!

Kids:

Now, look here, Jeremiah.
You're supposed to know what's right,
And you claim your words are good,
But you sit in prison like a hood
And tell your people not to fight!
Good night!

You deserve to be in prison
If you have such silly plans
About saving all the enemy
By falling in his hands!

Well, listen, Jeremiah,
We're not your fans,
Not anymore.
We can tell you that's not right,
Watching TV on the floor.

Why, sure!

Are you kidding, Jeremiah?
Did you flip your prophet's lid?
God doesn't say, "Surrender, kids!"
To kids like us, like that.

He doesn't give the cue
When we face the communists!
If anyone gives in to them,
He's just a dirty rat.

Your way of fighting, Jeremiah,
Just doesn't suit God's men.
If we believe that God's with us,
Why make a fuss
And be a bunch of chickens?

And then you try to tell us
That when you had a hunch,
Eating lunch,
Starving there in prison,
Your hunch was really God.

Hot dog!

Well, we have had a bunch of hunches,
And we've been reeling round with feelings,
But we never say, "Hey, kids, it's God!"
Every time
Our intuition's running wild,
Teen-age style.

How can you be sure, Uncle Jeremiah,
That you aren't a little queer
When you buy a strip of land
And say,
"God planned it so
To be a hangout for His sons"?

Way to go!

Are you fooling, Jeremiah?
Do you really mean to say
That we are asked to follow dreams
Like yours?

Do you want a glib "Amen!"
Or a sassy kind of "Yes!"
To that special bit about new men
Who know exactly how God feels
And exactly what to do?

Big deal!

We are all baptized,
And we've been around the town,
But we don't seem
To know our God
According to the dream,
That wild fantastic dream
Of poor old Jeremiah.

No one ever said
That we could bring God in
As a member of our gang,
As a guy who could be trusted
And treated like a man.

God is way out there,
And He doesn't hang around
The way we like to do.

And this brand-new covenant of God
Is supposed to be a plan
Where everyone is perfect
And knows God man to man?

Man, oh, man, oh, man!

We could never be like that!
We could never make the grade.
We are normal!
We are real!
Don't try and make us phonies.
Don't try and make us feel
As if we should be holy joes.

We'd never make it, Jeremiah!
God only knows!

> *Are you fooling, Jeremiah?*
> *Aren't you rather out of line?*
> *For we don't know our God like that,*
> *Not kids like us, like that.*
>
> *God doesn't change His men*
> *According to a plan*
> *Where every kid is perfect,*
> *Now I ask you, man to man.*
>
> *Your brand-new covenant, Jeremiah,*
> *May be quite a dream,*
> *But you can't find a modern man,*
> *With wheel in hand*
> *To keep up steam, like that.*

The Lord:
I'm getting rather tired
Of the way you kids respond
To the dreams and hopes
Of My prophet Jeremiah!
You're the dopes!

Why jump on Jeremiah?
Why beat him in the ground?
Don't you ever dream
Or have high expectations?
Have you ever tried
To understand
Just where God's plan was going?

For I, you see,
I am the Way,
The Hope of Jeremiah.
I am the Dream,
The Life of his tomorrow,
The new Bond,
The new Cord,
The new Covenant
That unites new men with God.

But all of this won't mean a thing
Until you see your prison,
Until you hear the verdict
That hangs above your life
As you swing from day to day
And game to game
Around your vicious, little circle,
That maypole called yourself!

I see you breaking ties
The way that Judas did,
Breaking ties with friends,
With guys that make you mad,
With girls who have a fad,
With teachers,
And with adults everywhere.
I see you breaking ties,
Fraying bonds
That your parents try to knit.
You know the flip way

You treat the family at home.
You know,
And so do I!

I see you cutting cords,
The links of love
That others forged for you.
I see you breaking ties
The way that Peter did,
Denying Me,
Because you're thinking of yourself.
I see you pampering yourself,
Cuddling yourself,
Getting for yourselves,
Loving to yourselves
Even when you're kissing others.

I see you breaking ties,
The very tie of life with God,
By trying to extract from life
All the tasty juices
Until it dies
Before you reach the age of twenty-five.

For every time
You break a tie
Or harm someone inside
By the way you act
Or what you say,
You have split the cord of love
And torn the tie with God a little more,
That covenant of life
That He has spun with thorns
And nails and blood at Calvary.

If for a moment
You can feel yourself alone,
Torn free from all the moorings,
Cut off from all the ties
With men and God
That give life meaning —
If you can see your selfish self
Floating off alone
Because you only love your world
Instead of loving others,
Then perhaps the dream
Of a new bond made by God,

A new covenant of life
Which you certainly don't deserve,
May not be quite so strange.

So if you're not too proud,
Too busy,
Or too old,
I will throw you My forgiveness
As I did when men like you
Were coldly nailing Me
To the splintered stake of death.
My forgiveness reaches out
As you hear Me cry, "You're in,"
As you see Me sweat and die
For all the broken ties
Between mankind and God.

Because I bring forgiveness,
I really bring you God,
And I become the new Tie,
The new Cord,
The new Covenant
Binding you to God as new men,
Freed men,
My men.

And this new tie
Ties up with other men,
Forgiving and living
With men and kids
Who are on the skids
As they so often are.

For this new cord
Means binding wounds—
And that can often mean
That you must suffer in the process
As you, like Me,
Put forgiveness into action,
Learning to accept
When you have been forgiven,
And learning how
To give yourselves from Me
So that you can show forgiveness,
Hope, and love.

In a way
Your life can be
A happening with hands
Reaching out,
Taking hold,
Hanging on,
Feeling others,
Sensing love from Me.

I'm waiting for you
To take My forgiveness
And mend the ties
That you have broken
And others too have broken.
I'm waiting!
I'm waiting for you!
I'm waiting.

Let's celebrate!

part two

*A Prayer with Those Who
Find It Hard to Love*

THERE ARE SOME PEOPLE I DON'T EVEN WANT TO LOVE

FoR CHRiST's SAKE

My Lord,
I'm sure that You must realize by now
That You are asking me to do the impossible.
At least, it's impossible for me.
I can't love other people all the time.
I have trouble loving myself sometimes.
Other people are different
Or disgusting
Or dull
Or dirty.
And I hate dirty people.
They make me sick.
There are some people I don't even want to love
Or like
Or help
Or understand
Or go through the agony of forgiving.
They do things to annoy me.
Or they get on my nerves and gall me
Till they make me mad.
Others are really enemies.
Do You understand, God, my enemies?
How can I love people the way that You demand,
Giving myself at their expense,
Forgetting about my own needs to rescue them?
It's impossible.
And yet You say that people who do not love
Do not know God.
Don't I know You, God?
I want to know You.
If You can love me all the way,
If You can surrender Yourself into my hands,
If You can give Yourself to die for me,
Yes, if You can love like that,
You must be God, I think.
But I can't see You,
And I can't love,
And I can't seem to find the new day,
The new age when love is all victorious,
When all men know the Lord
Instinctively, as Jeremiah says.
Maybe I hate Jeremiah too.

I strive to pose a front,
A masquerade of holy love, kindness, and

Of community concern for others,
For the ugly and the idiot,
But I know the sham I have created,
And so do You.
You tell me all that Christ has done.
You say, "Look, there is love."
I see and say, "Amen,"
But after that I fall.

For Christ's sake,
Help me.

I need another step,
I need a lift,
I need a power,
I need something more
Than this image of perfect suffering,
Of Christ the love of God
Hanging on my wall.

I need You, God, within me.
I need some love power driving me,
Driving me to love,
To forgive
And forgive
And to accept forgiveness from those I cannot love.

Can You make me Christ, God?
Can You?

Please, God, may others who have loved
Show me that power now to love the loveless
And the dying,
To forgive the unforgivable
And the lying,
Before it is too late.

Tie me to Christ,
And make me over again.

For Christ's sake, God!
For Christ's sake!